Eyes open to sexual abuse

What every parent needs to know

Written and illustrated by Nina Burrowes

Published by NB Research Ltd
First Floor, 80 Haymarket
London
SW1Y 4TE

© Nina Burrowes 2014

The disclaimer bit
I am not a clinician. I am not a child psychologist. This book contains my thoughts and opinions
about sexual abuse. Some of this is based on empirical evidence. Some of it is not.
I recommend that as well as reading this book you seek other advice and come to your own
decisions about what is right for you and your family.

But if you want my thoughts... here they are.

Get in touch to find out how your organisation can
earn money by being a stockist of my books.

www.ninaburrowes.com

I create books, videos, and cartoons that help people understand sexual abuse.

That's me in one of my videos!

I've created this guide for parents because when it comes to sexual abuse...

Your ignorance is the greatest risk your child faces

Opening our eyes to the realities of sexual abuse isn't easy.

I know quite a lot about sexual abuse, but this knowledge doesn't always make me feel safer.

There is a difference between <u>feeling</u> safe and <u>being</u> safe. Often the more I know, the more uncomfortable I feel.

But our knowledge is how we protect our kids.

So let's choose to learn more, even if it feels
a bit uncomfortable.

Facts and figures

The first thing you need to know is how to be a
smart consumer of the numbers.

We have some great information...

...but there's a lot that we don't know
Hmmm. I think I need a bigger crowbar!
THE BLACK BOX OF SEXUAL ABUSE

We don't have good information on crimes that are never reported or on victims who never seek help.

But for now we need to be aware that we don't have all the information.

With that in mind, let's look at what we <u>do</u> know.

What is 'sexual abuse'?

Grooming a child for sexual abuse.

Exposing a child to pornography.

Using a child to create indecent images.

Encouraging a child to watch or engage
in masturbation.

Touching a child sexually or encouraging
a child to engage in sexual touch.

Penetration of a child's mouth,
anus or vagina.

How many children are abused?

8% of boys under 18

20% of girls under 18

Those are both BIG numbers.

No child is immune from sexual abuse.

Children in all countries, of all ethnicities, classes, and religions are sexually abused.

Sexual abuse is in our communities, schools, clubs, friendship groups and families.

Check the facts - see reference 1

At what age are children at risk?

The short answer is 'any age'.

As our children get older and become young
adults the risk shifts into risk of relationship
violence, sexual assault and rape.

We need to give our children tools for life.
Tools that they can teach their own kids too.

Who are the abusers?

The boxes below are to scale

Person known
by the child but
not a member
of the family.

(a friend, neighbour
or professional)

A member of
their family

A stranger

The smallest group of abusers are strangers.

Which leads to the question...

? If our children are at least
risk of abuse by strangers
why do we spend so much time
teaching them about the
danger of strangers? ?

Because it's comforting to think that we could
teach our kids a simple rule that would keep
them safe from sexual abuse.

How to stay safe
Step 1 of 1

1. AVOID STRANGERS

It's comforting. But it's not true

Because it's comforting to think that sex offenders are very easy to spot.

It's comforting. But it's not true

Because it's comforting to think that no one we know could possibly be a danger to our children.

It's comforting. But it's not true

Focusing on the danger of strangers is a classic case of parents avoiding the uncomfortable truth at the expense of the actual safety of their kids.

When we focus on strangers...

So let's learn some uncomfortable truths and put the 'stranger danger' message into perspective.

A sex offender is most likely to be male but they can also be female. They can be young or old, from any ethnicity, class, or religion.

They can be taxi drivers, teachers, executives, psychologists or class mates.

They can be single or married, heterosexual or gay. They can be parents, grandparents, or have no children of their own.

When we focus on strangers we miss a very important point - attacking a child that they do not know is a high-risk strategy for an offender.

Sex offenders know that their offending is far less likely to be detected if they target children they already have access to.

To find out more about this watch my video 'Why are sex offenders able to get away with it' on YouTube.

Focusing on strangers distracts our kids from the greater risks

When it comes to road-safety we teach our children to look left and right.

We teach them to cross at the crossing

Have you ever taught your child what to do if a drunk-driver mounts the pavement and is closing in on them at speed?

No. Why??Because whilst this <u>could</u> happen
the risk is low compared to the other dangers.

Because if that scenario did happen there is very
little your child could do to protect themselves.

And because teaching your child about that risk
may undermine some of the other safety messages.

Only teaching our kids about the danger of strangers is like teaching them to avoid the drunk driver without ever teaching them how to cross the road.

We need to equip our kids for the risks they are more likely to face.

I have one more uncomfortable truth to share with you. It will be hard to hear but it will help to place the 'stranger danger' message into perspective.

Remember...

Your child is three times more likely to be abused by another child than an adult stranger

Around 30% of child sexual abuse is perpetrated by children.

We don't tend to talk about this aspect of abuse because it is particularly uncomfortable. But this is another example of placing our comfort above the actual safety of our kids.

We need to have the courage to change that.

Children who sexually abuse children

This shouldn't be confused with the normal sexual development of our kids. Below is a table that gives you an idea of age-appropriate sexual behaviours.

Age in years

0 - 4	5 - 9	10 - 12	13 - 16
Curiosity about body parts		'Dating' and kissing other children	Experimenting sexually with children of the same age
Playing games with other children that involve exploring the body			
		Looking for sexual images on the internet	
Displaying, touching, or rubbing genitals for comfort		Masturbating in private	

Source: www.nspcc.org.uk

Some children, such as those with learning difficulties, are likely to show a different development pattern to this.

1. Sexual abuse is paid-forward

The vast majority of people who are sexually abused do <u>not</u> go on to abuse anyone else.

But, <u>some</u> people who are abused do go on to abuse others and sometimes this happens in childhood.

For some children this happens because they do not realise that what happened to them was abuse. They did not meet the scary stranger that their parents had warned them about.

The abuse may have been introduced as a game by someone they like.

And so they do what they do with other games, they introduce it to the other children they know.

Research suggests that only 1% of victims of child sexual abuse are later charged with committing a sex offence themselves.
Check the facts - see reference 5

Some children <u>do</u> realise that what happened
to them was abuse.

They can respond to their feelings of betrayal,
shame, anger, and fear by acting out the
abusive behaviours they have experienced
on the children around them.

2. Children who are paedophiles

Paedophilia is a sexual attraction to
children who have not gone through puberty.
Paedophiles can be exclusively attracted to
children or they can be attracted to children
as well as people of their own age.

As with other types of sexual attraction,
people can realise that they are attracted to
children anytime from early adolescence.

Paedophiles first realise that they are
sexually attracted to children.

And then they have a choice...

To act on this
attraction and
commit a sex
offence

To find a way
of managing
this attraction
so that they
never offend

It's in everybody's interest that young people
who realise that they are attracted to children
get all the support they need.

3. Teenagers and sex

Another reason why young people are sexually abusing each other is because we're not talking to our teenagers about sex and relationships.

This gap is being filled by pornography.

These films and images do not cover the issue of consent. Consent happens off-camera.

This means that young people are not learning how to ensure they have consent. They may 'assume' that they have it.

They may also have skewed ideas of what types of sexual activity is and is not 'normal' in the early stages of a young relationship. All of this can mean that their early sexual encounters are aggressive and abusive.

And so the big question is

How do I keep my child safe?

If there was a way to eliminate the risk of sexual abuse I would...

But as with most of the risks your child faces it's a case of

REDUCING

risk rather than eliminating it.

You need to be realistic about what is possible. The areas where parents can have a big impact are:

Let's take a look at detecting abuse…

Is someone a potential abuser?

Signs to look for in a potential abuser

Very interested in the sexual development of your child

Talks about or to your child in a sexual way

Touches your child excessively. Does not stop even if your child does not appear to be enjoying it.

Insists on being alone with your child and does not like to be interrupted

Appears to be infatuated with your child

Spends more time with your child than people of their own age

Manufactures opportunities to be alone with your child

Attempts to isolate your child emotionally by having a 'special' relationship with them

Gives your child gifts for no reason

Gives your child a mobile phone or seeks other ways to communicate with them that exclude you

Remember, the presence of these signs does not necessarily mean that someone _is_ an abuser and the absence of these signs does not necessarily mean that they <u>are not</u> an abuser.

What if I suspect someone?

If you feel that someone is a potential threat to your child do not dismiss this instinct.

Your instinct could mean nothing. You could be picking up on something that has nothing to do with abuse. Your instinct could have more to do with you than them.

But with a great deal of compassion for the person in question (remember, they could well be completely innocent) limit the nature of the contact that they have with your child.

It wouldn't be fair to place them in a situation where they could be accused of something they didn't do. So don't let that situation arise.

If this person is a close friend or family member you need to find a balance between keeping this person in your child's life and making sure your child is safe.

Don't ask them to babysit but do still invite them into your home when you are there to supervise their visit.

If there is a particular behaviour that makes you feel uncomfortable (e.g. touching) talk to them about it and explain that you are teaching your child about body choice and respect.

It would be unfair of you to discuss your concern with a large number of people. But do talk to someone who knows both of you and see if they share your concerns.

If you still have concerns then seek expert advice. Search on the internet for helplines that will offer 'advice about suspected child abuse.'

Spotting abuse

Displays age-inappropriate sexual behaviour, language, or knowledge

For example
Acting out sex acts with toys

Tries to avoid or seems reluctant to spend time with certain people

Signs to look for in your child

Bruising, any marks around the genitals, signs of sexually transmitted diseases, pregnancy.

Withdrawn, problems at school, regressed behaviour such as bed wetting, sleeping or eating problems, anxiety, sudden changes in behaviour, self-harm, use of drugs or alcohol.

Remember, the presence or absence of these signs does not mean that abuse is or is not taking place.

The uncomfortable reality that I live with is this:

Someone I know could be an abuser. I would not expect to be able to 'spot' it.

A child I know could be being abused. I would not expect to be able to 'spot' it.

Living with this truth is uncomfortable, but it means that I am never blinded by my own assumptions.

Opening your eyes to the realities of sexual abuse is a balancing act.

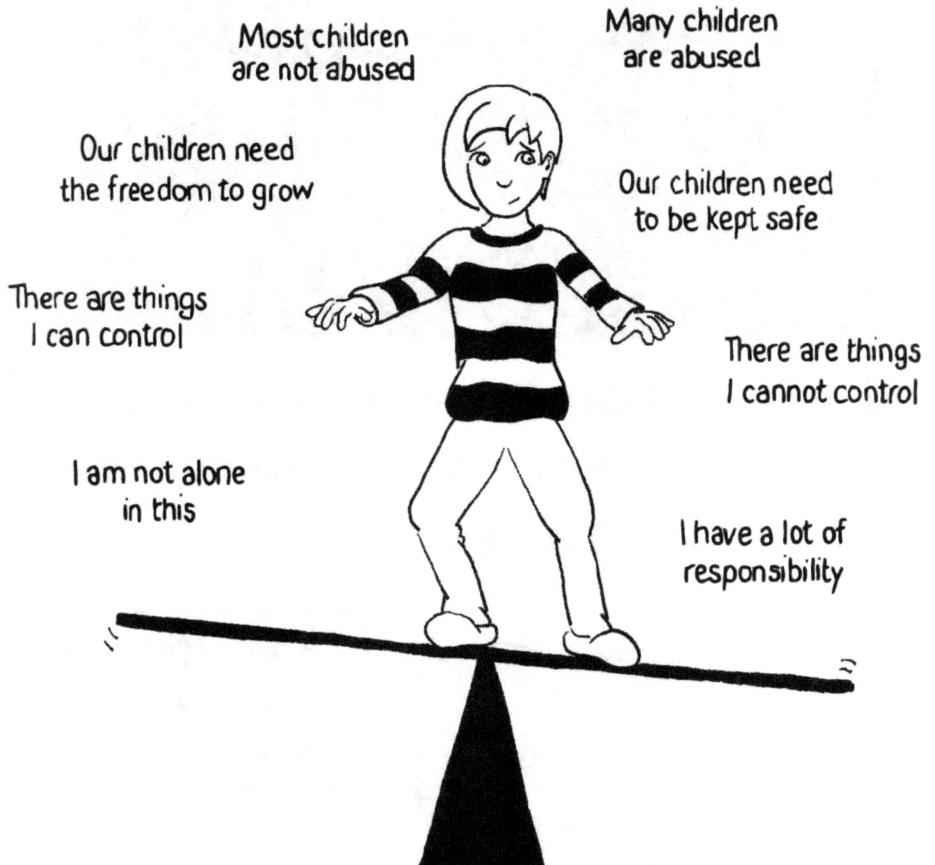

Every now and then it's worth asking yourself if you think you're getting the balance right.

Which means it's also important to look after yourself when you're learning about abuse.

How are you doing?

Time for a break?

Coming next - So what can you do?

So what can you do?

Much of the advice given to parents about abuse places the emphasis on what the child should or should not do.

We fail to realise how confusing these messages can be to children and how much our own behaviour can undermine the messages.

So my advice is based on these principles:

1. You are a role model

The emphasis of my
advice is on what y<u>ou</u>
need to do. Not what
your child needs to do.

2. There is no 'quick fix'

Living with the risks of abuse is complex.
A few simple rules aren't enough. This is
something you need to include as part of
your parenting and grandparenting forevermore.

3. Your child is an adult in the making

You're not raising a child. You're raising an adult.

Which means we need to give our children tools that will also help them in adulthood.

And we need to make sure that as well as protecting children from abuse we also raise adults who are confident around other people, comfortable about their bodies and comfortable about sex.

So let's learn how to do that...

We can't rely on children to recognise that they are being sexually abused. So we need to help them understand what abuse is in a way that won't frighten them.

Teach young children that the parts of their body that are covered by their underpants are special.

I can touch myself here

Children shouldn't play games with anyone else that involves touching here

Teach your children how to wash their own bodies. Give them a sense of pride that they can do it themselves.

I can do it myself!

I don't need anyone else to help!

Don't make my body a mystery to me

It's important that our children grow up knowing their own bodies. Teach your children the correct words for all of their body parts.

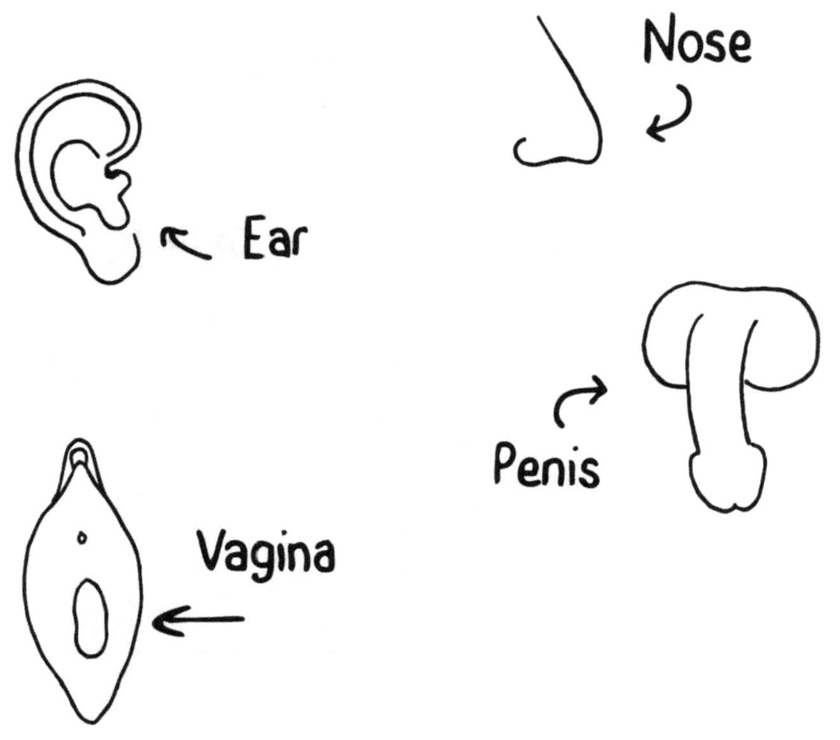

Be 'matter of fact' about this because it _is_ a matter of fact.

Parents can feel too embarrassed to talk about sexual organs with their children. Often this is an embarrassment they were taught by their own parents.

Let's not pay this shame forward onto another generation.

Especially because ignorance makes your child more susceptible to abuse.

How can your daughter tell you that someone has touched her vagina if she never knew she had one, she doesn't have a word for it, and she's confused about whether she SHOULD have one?

Answer questions about bodies truthfully.
You might not always know the answer,
so find out together.

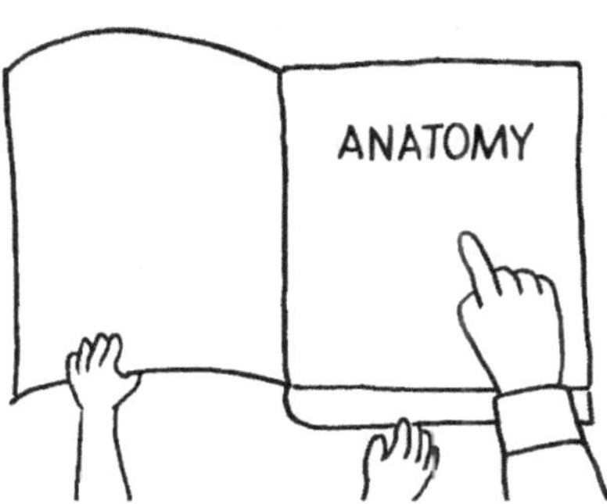

As your children get older help them find
resources where they can get healthy
answers about sex and relationships.

Search online for
'sex advice
website teenagers'

If your children have always got accurate,
honest, and full answers from you they are less
likely to turn to other sources of information.

Help your child learn that they get to make choices about their own body and that those choices should be respected by other people.

If you are tickling a child and they ask you to stop. Then stop.

I may be laughing but I'm also learning that when I say 'stop' I can't expect people to do what I want. Especially if they are bigger and stronger than me.

If your child does not want to kiss someone help them learn that it is okay to say 'no'
Be a good girl and kiss Granny goodbye
I don't want to
If you force me to show affection I'll learn that I don't get to choose who I kiss and that I should always give in to pressure from others.

Role-model these lessons for your child by being the kind of family that respects each other's body choices.

Most parents assume that their kids can tell them anything.

This isn't a safe assumption.

Think of all the things you never told your parents.

Being able to have the difficult conversations is like everything else in life that's difficult.

It takes practice.

Be a role model for your kids by showing them it's okay to share how you're feeling.

Be a role model at listening as well as talking.

Every time you…

React angrily

Seem distracted

Hmmm Yep. Hmmm. I'm listening.

Dismiss what they are saying

Oh don't be silly!

…is a backward step for the big conversation they might need to have with you one day.

Making mistakes is part of the process.

These moments can turn out to be valuable lessons too.

I'm sorry. I wasn't angry at you.
I think I was just a bit scared.

I'm sorry I wasn't really listening.
That was rude of me. Tell me again.
You've got all of my attention this time.

I'm sorry. It's not silly.
You must think that a lot of
the things I worry about are silly.

It's inevitable that one day your child will
be worried about telling you something.

So why not plan ahead?

When I was a child our family would talk about
what we would do if there was a fire at home.

It was a good way of mentally rehearsing what
we would do if this frightening situation arose.

I know what to do!

You can do the same for the difficult
conversations in life.

Talk to your child about what you could
do if either of you had something
difficult to share.

You may find that they would feel more
comfortable writing you a letter or talking
to someone else first.

By having this conversation you'll already be
showing your willingness to listen.

And you'll be showing them that it's normal to
have things that are difficult to talk about.

Finally, if your child is trying to tell you
something

Believe them

Not being believed by the people who are
supposed to protect you can cause just
as much harm as the original abuse and
it leaves your child wide open to further abuse.

Of course you won't want it to be real.
But don't let this make you willfully
deaf to what they are saying.

At an <u>absolute minimum</u> investigate the
facts but believe that what they are
saying feels real to them.

Make sure they feel heard and believed.

Becoming a trusted person to share life's challenges with is one of the greatest gifts you can give your child.

But that kind of relationship doesn't just happen automatically.

You need to consciously choose to build it.

Let's do a quick recap before I point you towards some more resources.

As a parent you need to...

1. Have the courage to open your eyes to the real risks

2. Never assume that...

You'll be able to spot an abuser
You'll be able to tell if your child is being abused
Your child will tell you if something is wrong

3. Be a role model for...

Body choice
Body respect
Talking and listening

Check out my online video series where I answer your questions about sexual abuse.

You'll find videos about supporting someone who has been abused, therapy, and information about perpetrators.

You can also submit your question for me to answer.

Read my illustrated book about life after abuse.

The courage to be me

A story of courage, self-compassion and hope
after sexual abuse

By Dr Nina Burrowes

This book will help you understand some
of the challenges that people who have
been abused face.

You can read it in full for free
on my website or buy a copy for yourself.

Visit www.ninaburrowes.com

Academic research on sexual abuse

If you'd like to read more academic research on sexual abuse then search for this online. Many organisations have links to research reports or you can use search tools like Google Scholar.

To read my research on sexual abuse visit my research website.

Visit www.nb-research.com

Finding more help online

There are lots of organisations around the world that will offer you advice and support about sexual abuse.

Search online using phrases like 'help, information, advice, helpline' and 'abuse, child sexual abuse or rape'

If you can't find what you're looking for phone one of the helplines - they may be able to point you in the right direction.

How can I make a difference?

Most communities have charities
that support people who have
been raped or sexually abused.

These organisations are over-worked
and under-funded.

They are also invisible - until you need them.

They need their local community to support them.
They need help with fundraising, campaigning
and awareness raising.

Ensure the future survival of your local
agency by making contact with them and
seeing how you can support their work.

Reducing the impact of sexual abuse
is _everybody's_ job.

Thank you for buying my book.

By doing so you're helping me continue to create content about sexual abuse.

I try to keep a large proportion of my content free to access.

Somewhere out there are people who need information.

And they can't necessarily afford to pay for it.

My friend has told me her boyfriend raped her. I don't know what to do...

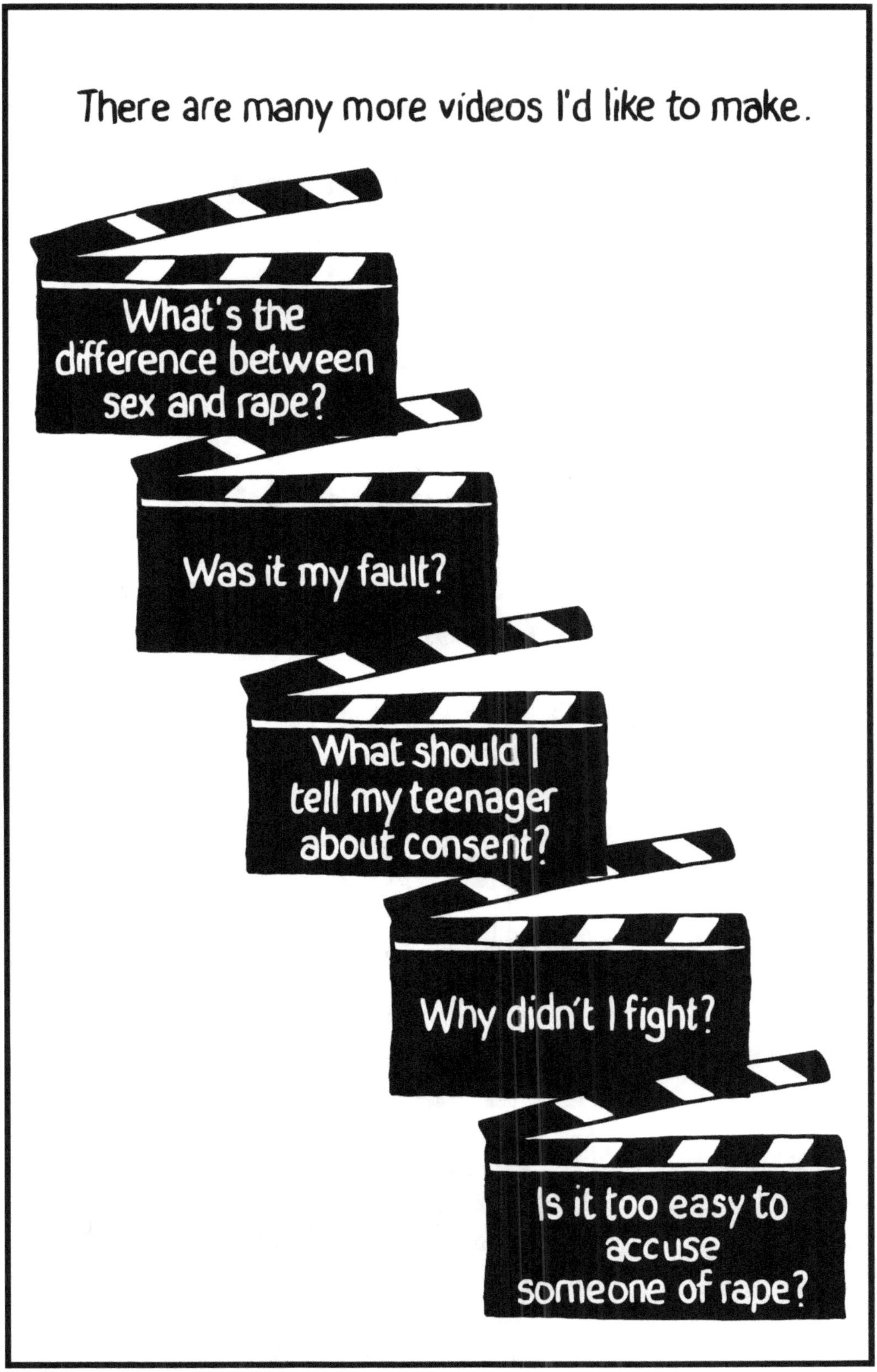

There are many more videos I'd like to make.
What's the difference between sex and rape?
Was it my fault?
What should I tell my teenager about consent?
Why didn't I fight?
Is it too easy to accuse someone of rape?

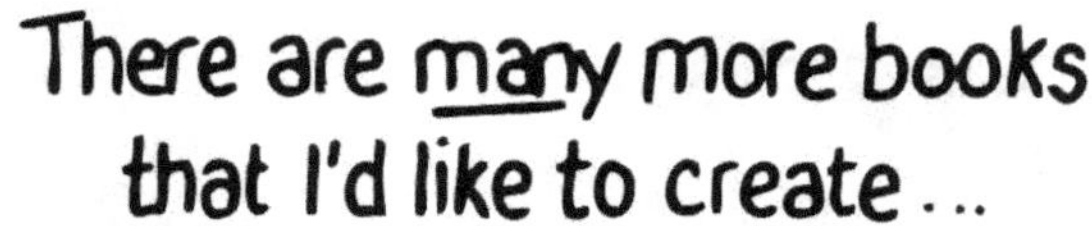

There are many more books
that I'd like to create ...

The psychology of good sex.
What every teenager needs to know.
Sex after sexual abuse
Supporting a child who has been sexually abused.
A guide for parents.

By buying this one you're helping
to make that happen.

Thank you!

I'm a research psychologist who specialises in the psychology of sexual abuse.

I look at sexual abuse with a wide lens.

I take complex research and turn it into content that is easier to understand.
BURROWES

Some of my work helps people understand sexual abuse better...

Some of my work helps people understand
the path towards a solution...

To find out more about me and my work visit

www.ninaburrowes.com

References

I have tried to use research sources that you'll be able to find yourself online. Search for the article title to find the full source.

1. Pereda, N., Guilera, G, Forns, M. + Gomez-Benito, J. (2009). The prevalence of child sexual abuse in community and student samples: A meta-analysis. *Clinical Psychology Review, 29(4),* 328-338.

2. Douglas, E. + Finkelhor, D. (2005). Childhood Sexual Abuse Factsheet. [Online] www.unh.edu/ccrc/factsheet/pdf/CSA-FS20.pdf

3. Vizard, E. (2013). The victims and juvenile perpetrators of child sexual abuse. Assessment and intervention. *Journal of Clinical Psychology and Psychiatry,* 54(5), 503-515.

4. 'Healthy sexual behaviour in children and young people' at www.nspcc.org.uk

5. The issue of a 'cycle of abuse' is contentious and research shows varying trends. This study is pretty comprehensive: Ogloff, J., Cutajar, M., Mann, E., + Mullen, P. (2012). Child sexual abuse and subsequent offending and victimisation: A 45 year follow-up study. Trends and issues in crime and criminal justice, No. 440 Available at www.aic.gov.au/media_library/publications/tandi_pdf/tandi440.pdf

Other titles by Nina Burrowes

The courage to be me

The little book on authenticity

Coming soon

The little book on choice